Veil On, Veil Off

poems by

John Marcus Powell

EXOT BOOKS
2018

www.exottreasures.com/exotbooks

Copyright 2018 EXOT BOOKS
All Rights Reserved
Typeset in Iowan Old Type & Copperplate
ISBN: 978-0-9898984-3-0

Illustrations & Design: Julio M. Perea
Editor: R Nemo Hill

Acknowledgments

The Author wishes to thank those publications
in which versions of these poems originally appeared.

John Hopkins Review
Writing
Lovers On The Roof
The River

The Village Voice
Quentin Crisp In Public Transit

Photograph by — Ajna J. Lichau   John Marcus Powell & Walter Cox — June 2017

These poems are dedicated to

WALTER COX

I see a beautiful gigantic swimmer swimming naked
    through the eddies of the sea,
His brown hair lies close and even to his head,
    he strikes out with couraguous arm, he urges himself with his legs.

WALT WHITMAN

CONTENTS

FOR THE BIRDS

Wake-Up Call	1
Conductor	2
Mahler's Wife	4
Dancing Classes	6
For The Birds	9
Organ Music	12
Cloaked	14
Actress	15
Out With Friends	17
True Voice	19
Background Music	21

EVIDENT BED

Love On The Roof	25
Missed Connections	29
Gone Wild	31
Street Scenes	33
Looking For Bottoms	35
Masseur	38
Cruising	41
Meeting	45
Straight Talk	47
One Two Three	49
Hotel	50

RIVER

To Walk The Walk	55
River	57
Naked Nudes	59
Peace	61
Bicycle Thief	63
Lost Poem	65
Flood	67
Earthquake	70
Nudes On Brighton Beach	72
Tattoos	74
Jail Or Rehab	76

THE FULL SKETCH

Jock Doc	81
Angry Romanian Surgeon	83
Bank Manager	85
Unemployed In Philly	87
The Full Sketch	90
Nouns Must Go	93
Boy's War	95
Quentin Crisp In Transport	97
I Was Eighteen Virginia Years	99
Door Taps	103

O virgins, demons, monsters, martyrs all,
Great Spirits scornful of reality,
Who seek the infinite, believers, trulls,
Enraptured, or in utter misery.

Charles Baudelaire

For The Birds

WAKE-UP CALL

Lovers and Enemies wake up tender.
Fumbling into the day's first speak, the body mumbles
"I'm alive! This is a treat!"
And the haze of dawn fades into a clarity.

Except, at this morning's dawn, my partner's sleep is
interrupted by a chicken.
This *cock-a-doodle* takes some deciphering
for in the pale light it's less *cock-a-doodle* than *kara-kara-kara*.
My partner whispers,
"Some idiot is keeping a fucking rooster on a balcony."
So I raise the blind—

and at apartment windows
are city dwellers with binoculars,
and on the roof of a clinic
are nurses with thermometers.
Kara-kara-kara has so wounded the awakening
that security guards cock their weapons,
therapists return to Freudian dissertations,
and at a prison on the periphery
the executioner double-checks the electric chair.

As my partner yearns for sleep
there's a shout: "The damn thing's flying!"
But nothing has been sighted,
it's a false alarm

—and *kara-kara-kara* continues,
an articulation under marmalade colored feathers
expressing an ability to take off o'er fences,
to view civilization from aerials and weather vanes
and branches.

And the perfection of the coxcomb,
that straggle of red each side the beak
will be the accompanying visual, signaling—"Too late!
Too late to save the orchestral energy of streams
(never mind the rivers)!
Complications are arising
despite unrelenting visits
to your outrageously expensive gym!"

Conductor

After studying piano
and orchestration and composition and musical history,
we are given tickets
(we study at different schools
with different famous teachers)
to a concert in an outer borough
with flesh and blood musicians.
The program is two symphonic moderns
with a rare chamber piece between.

The conductor is a radical.
His radicalism pierces the spirit.
The spirit shakes the body,
so all the bodies of all the audience will hump all the brains.
For the peppering of such an evening,
insanity is essential.
"Please let the evening not be sane!"

In the uptown apartment
we are introduced.
We are severely beautiful.
We are academic.
We analyze symphonies,
and are considered possible conductors,
i.e. dictators of the truth.
Here comes the composer philanthropist
who arranged the proceedings.
"Let's get cracking, get to know each other.
Let's take the subway
and change at 14th street."

We tangle.
We are a ball rolling,
a heap of lovers
withstanding the upsy-daisy
of the ball's turning.

But on the 14th street platform
of Union Square Station
we become over-anxious.
Have the orchestral authorities been informed?

Are they anticipating our arrival?
Can we grab each cultural moment
with sufficient upturned eye-ball?
Is this the correct platform
with the correct line for the correct train?

The fear is only the ingestion
of an absence of formulae in an over-crowded station.
So we roll on to the concert hall
to sit with strangers in isolation
and watch the stage
where rehearsed accidents are being traced.

This is the tuning-up,
the before happening explanation
of arriving before travelling—
illustration of the conjuror's tricks.

A homo-hetero oboist
ogles a hetero-homo timpanist.
They smell out musical phrasing
like buffalo who are friends.
Bass-men in the basement
honk a rhythm of biking donkey camels.
Upstairs, antic cellists preen slender necks.
When violins violas woodwinds open up their scores
they are not hankering after a better coming after.
They are content
with one note
then one phrase
as sweet complete.

And this is only preparation!
A conductor would be a tattered condom
on a fine thick dick,
a sex worker who arrives hours after the orgasm
in the demolished building,
an over stimulator of the metaphysical tit.

This tuning-up is gorgeous, haunting.
Do we need a conductor?
Do we need a concert?
We're not sure—yet!

Mahler's Wife

Alma, a composer, marries Gustav Mahler.
She's wide open to history and is twenty.
He's a geezer past forty,
inside a sturdy Austrian home.

"You'll have to stop writing music.
In this marriage there is room for only one composer.
My works take up both our energies.
My intention is to produce a symphony about the
'Resurrection'.
All told there'll be 9 to 10 symphonic smackeroos."

Alma's hypnotized by the wallpaper
that seals the conjugal covenant
in the bedroom bathroom dining room
study and living rooms.

Gustav Mahler relents when Alma miscarries.
"The baby you birthed lived a very short while.
This has left you depressed.
Write a few beautiful songs."

Before the marriage Alma had written wonderful songs.
But, talented as Alma is, it has to be inspirational.
After she's been instructed to cut it off,
she can't just suddenly turn it on.

De toute façon, shortly after,
Mahler gets a fever.
As quick as a quick sonata
the blue birds from the bathroom wallpaper sing,
"Gustav's dead. Gustav's gone."

Alma modulates towards other gentlemen.
An architect. A poet.
A Polish painter with a dreadful Polish name.
Relationships are consummated—
as long as the painter paints her,
the architect design houses
that in their modernism are inspired by her,

the poet enables her to be recognized
as a voyager on the poetic main.

If you were a sanitation worker or a construction worker
she wanted nothing to do with you.
But on her way back from visiting the poet,
she leaves her chauffeur in the car
intending to pop into a bar,
and runs into a storm
gulping up the scene.

Alongside her,
houses are blown inside out,
the wallpaper on the inside
is on the outside,
blue birds from bathroom walls
screech round and round.

Alma sits in the bar
while a disordered wind whines
a discordant Armageddon
and in scary turmoil
produces a song cycle

without
gender
in E flat minor
without
I or me or thee or thou.

Dancing Classes

In the late 40s
ex-soldiers working in factories
take their wives dancing
in the ballroom of the Greyhound Hotel.

Uncle Eric
who'd soldiered in Africa,
now working at a factory
that makes *nylon fiber*
(when the world war raged
nylon had been rare)
has the glide of a fish at its silvery best.
He excels at the Foxtrot,
the Quickstep slowed.

Uncle Eric is single,
eliciting partners.
He partners in general.
This is the age of dancing with partners,
negotiating an after-war life
in communal waters.

After the interval
I stand next the French Windows.
I am 12 years old.
A coal miner
fresh from the town of two brawny syllables
—brawny like testicles—*Brymawr*—
runs up the stairs to me
up in the ballroom
leaving his girlfriend
in the bowels of the bathroom
under the soil
downstairs.

It'll take her 10 minutes
to check her make up,
giving my coal miner
time to establish his presence
by his brilliantined hair.

On a strain of the waltz, he grabs me tight
tight into his tight stomach
and twirls
one two three
past pillared windows
where night has drawn curtains
past the stage
where the orchestra's frightened.

One two three
he would never do this
with his girlfriend present
his tight stomach tightens
as the waltz becomes graphic
and I don't want this dance to conclude.

But dancing changed
when a different music came into fashion.
I'm 18, earning a salary,
and pop into the Greyhound
to drink a couple of rums
to prepare for a jive
in the jumping night town hall.

A mix of Elvis's
Blue Suede Shoes
is a hunk of funk
and Dixie
and Swing
is rain that whistles
in the lushest warm.

When the trad band
comes from Newport
I leap to the rock,
non-intimacy displayed with a partner
stretched at long distance
at the end of her arms and mine.

But within the beat
it's four-four-time,
she rolls in close.

Then to prove ourselves rid
one of the other
as she flings away
I shift my pelvis
because I am Elvis
and education gives it the name
'skip jive'.

A while later in London
in a sea of compatriots
in a club scooped out of a tunnel,
so packed together
no dancing is visible
but plenty of moves out of sight—
the police raid the cellar
and we're taken to jail.
"OK you homos!
What was you doin?"
"Only dancing."
"I'll give a name to what you call dancing.
I'll call it the Groping Grind."

New York City 2015.
My friend
wants to know
if we can go jiving
in a city
where a Mayor called Guiliani
tore out the under-belly.
Mayor's coming after you,
contributing a modern bright blight.

"Do you want to go jiving?"
I answer I'd only embarrass him.
"What is the occasion of your retiring?"
"Well one moment I'm 60
the next I'm 70.
If I don't throw in the towel
when I reach 80,
then 90 might be the apt time."

For The Birds

1.
Sparrow

I'm in Seattle.
Arrived by air at 2PM Western Standard Time.

By the time I collect my luggage
meet my friends, travel into the city,

it's rush hour and I'm older
though younger than I'll ever be again.

I sip a coffee at a sidewalk café
and watch a white man

with a white bandage at the side of his head
pulling a large trunk.

He pulls as if the trunk has wheels.
It doesn't even have legs.

A bird sitting on the conical top
of a rusting advertising kiosk

(a Pacific North American
corruption of Parisian kiosks)

flies down to the sidewalk,
pecking seeds from the cracks.

Small brown bird. With persistence I discover
patches of grey and stripes of black.

It's the type of sparrow that knows it's a sparrow,
is attractive to other sparrows

and, if it's having a good day,
will allow itself to be attracted back.

Two posters are glued on the kiosk:
First—
>   *FELLOWS*
>   *ENJOY A NICE COCK*
>   *TAIL*
>   *OR TWO AT*
>   *THE PONY*

Then—
>   *MILITARY OUT OF PUBLIC SCHOOLS*

Brown bird hops, not concerned about
popping or not popping into *The Pony* later.

Never worrying which poster's underneath,
which poster's on top.

2.
Heron

What of the North West will I remember?
From Europe I come back troubled by too many humans
in too little space.
North Africa freaks with too much vista.
In the Northwest I like the intimate—bears at the roadside,
reflected mountains, soil in turmoil, looking down
through lakes.
But God Almighty! This is much too mighty!
I'll turn my attention to a bird instead.

I am leaning against a friend's car
parked in an immobile line of traffic
waiting to get on the ferry.
The pained traffic aches,
which has to do with destinies that are edgy.
I am edgy, though the purpose of my holiday is to be at ease.

In the middle of the bay is a heron on a post,
a heron posted outside a port,
maintaining its position without strain.
I've had similar moments when standing on a mountain
allowing the horizon to view me with disdain.
My friend exits his car to tell me herons do not express disdain,
they don't have feelings for or against.
>   Bollocks!

I'll anthropomorphize if I want to.
I believe nature puts on a show,
that the heron is not in sight before I arrive
that it comes to the bay on the day I'll be there—
that it knows.

3.
Rooks

Six black birds pose on the patio rail.
A purple flush to their feathers expresses
the confident superiority of belonging to a group.
Also their public life displays
desire for each other, and care.

Lynne, who is Polish and lives in the house,
tells me: "If I do something against them, shoo them,
or bad-mouth them,
they'll ascend to the sky bearing nuts
to smash down on my cranium—
then flutter/caw, caw/flutter
to teach me respect.
They come from the family *Corvidae*, genus *Corvus*.
Among the most intelligent of animals.
They are crows."

That doesn't fool me.
I come from Wales. Wales is full of them.
They hail from rookeries and are rooks.

Lynn's husband comes onto the patio. He's Native American,
Pacific North West Indian.
He's certain that crows made it over from Europe
but whether crows, rooks, magpies, or ravens,
they're aware our subject is them.
They think on the wing,
personal as Facebook, intricate as the web.

They're encouraging their brethren to shit on the house,
to caw while we're speaking,
to imitate our waddle as we walk round the lake.
Then Lynn puts out stale bread on the patio.
And they soften it in the birdbath
and cuzz and drink.

ORGAN MUSIC

In the middle of our century
as we wait to be accepted into university

the most interesting among us
is an organist.

He dexterously fuses Elvis, Frescobaldi, Bach
and Armstrong.

He's an eighteen year old academic, blessed with wisdom
and with heart.

As we wait for the results of our examinations
extra-curricular activities are given.

Our history teacher's contribution is a lecture
in which he annihilates Marx.

After finishing he wants us to give reasons why
communism is no answer.

Rick the organist says, "Sorry, I have a lot of preparation.
I'm playing in church."

And he leaves the class
to walk to the cavernous Baptist Chapel—

where—he sits before the multi-manuals
of the gold piped organ.

His feet on the pedals
are shoeless, sockless.

He resists the urge to be bollocks naked,
to let historic rawness meet raw wood and sound.

In our old age we recognize each other in Birmingham.
I say. "I hear you are a composer. . . . ."

He replies, "I'm an engineer.
But I play the organ when the opportunity allows."

Almodovar, The War Requiem,
the bankruptcy of the health service for starters.

Gay marriage, Phillip Glass, and the end of capitalism for afters.
As we writhe in this chaos Rick says,

"Excuse me. I have a lot of preparation.
I have to play in church."

And he beats it to the cathedral—
where—ascending to the organ he takes off socks and shoes,

then at last succumbing,
removes jacket shirt trousers old age underclothes.

In his prime state
he's able to bear this sermon:

TO ACHIEVE THE ETERNAL
WE MUST DO AS WE'RE TOLD.

In the rear view mirror above the organ
he sees me sitting in the congregation.

I can't see him
but recognize his scrawny nakedness infusing his improvisation

of 'Ain't Nothing But A Hound Dog'
re-imagined as a fugue.

Elvis, Rodgers and Hammerstein, Frescobaldi,
the Holy Spirit—

Ricks' lolloping bollocks personify the same miracle,
only different.

Rick got there quicker than the rest of us.
It only took him 80 years.

CLOAKED

At a showing of *Superman*, in the flickering lights
a film-goer yells, "That cloak flows and billows!
Such effeminacy should be effaced!"
                When, as a teenager, a P.E. teacher
                mimicked my suspicious vocal patterns,
                he curtailed my romantic ambition
                to go on vacation with a masculine thug.
And when, in church,
the deep tall bass who had worked in India
accused me of sashaying to the altar
to receive the bread and water,
he convinced me I had to be careful
about delivering blows to faith.
                The accumulative wisdom was that my coat
                must never be worn cloaked suggestively
                over the shoulders
                or I'd turn Queer like *Superman*.
                Lying in my coffin, I and my jacket
                would remain rigid, in function, in place.
But while waiting for my coffin, I fell for a studly reporter
and was lucky to land a job on the local paper.
                My stud always left the office with his coat
                draped. One day,
                off duty, he comes in to see me.
                In full lunch time he's wearing his coat
                like a flamboyant cape.
                I recognized the flamboyance,
                flourishing on Grecian vases
                where the erect chase the erect
                wearing a slither of myth.
Capes, of which Greeks possessed many,
were exchanged frequently, as nothing out of the ordinary.
                Caprice.

Actress

Early in her career
the actress's complexities
are compressed to simplicities:
"The nucleus of you
is your sexual vivacity,
to which the rest of you is attached."
Then in mid-career:
"In recent films you display signs of mortality.
You have a contract with the public
to retain your form and shape."

So she gravitates to the theatre.
In her One-Woman-Show
the front rows are taken out
for her Beauty to be appreciated
from away a ways.
The body, through the supposed transparency
of her gown, is rubber?
What does that matter?
—as long as spectators witness
her will towards glamor.
Glamor is nature's idea of play.

After the show she spends hours preparing,
cos outside the stage door a crowd is waiting.
The unforgiving street is so packed,
she has to be hoisted onto the roof of her Rolls Royce.
"She has plenty of youth," yodels the masked crowd.
"Her face is hope displayed."

But she betrays hope by losing her balance,
breaking both hips as she falls off the stage.
From her Paris apartment
her beauty is telegraphed to printing houses
to be made into posters for cinema foyers and bars
on all sides of all oceans.
In the poster she's a child of forty
performing the crucial duty
of maintaining physical grace.

Yet a poster gets fainter.
And when each poster is taken down,
the oblong where the poster had been
is paler than the surrounding paint.
That oblong veers towards yearning.
So—as film aficionados drink coffee
beneath that oblong,
they yearn for the widest spread
of their own glamorous wings,
ready for feisty flight.

Out With Friends

The LGBT parade

is beginning under the brows of a gathering storm.
Under the hint of tempests,
the paraders are getting together at Central Park,
then marching down.

Spectators

preparing for a variety of tableaux
are afraid, when they look in a diverse direction,
they're going to miss an activity
outside the vortex of their attention.

Eh!

—the beginning is visible!
Now they embrace the charge
that pulsates in hearts!
History strengthens the pulse of the heart
and they feel it now!

On 5th Avenue

the top of the parade is at the top of a hill.
Dykes On Bikes are grinding engines,
raising the fists of gender leaders.
The most energetic raise themselves
95 per cent off their vehicles.
They're going to raise hell past the end of the century.
Their haunches are *so* strong.

Oh!

In a struggled sudden there's rain as the sun illuminates.
A rainbow is taken as a eulogy
for the gay man, last month, shot in the face
for walking on an American street,
for being lovely loving, for being young.

The shower

spits remorse for the Lesbian couple
over in Europe who perished in a fire
when neighbors suggested it would be fun
to brutalize their home.
Umbrellas provide no protection
against executions happening everywhere,
most recently to male teenage lovers in Iran.

Oh! Listen!

—to the roar for the band
that plays bright
as the storm subsides.
This band that plays bright
has a knife-slender brown cheerleader.
With each chuck of his rod, he's older, he is tenderer.
When he can no longer chuck it, he'll sling it.
When he can't sling it, he'll sing it.
When he can't sing it, he'll prance beyond.

On 14th Street

two sequined males pose in the summer grey flakes.
My friend Parker takes photos.
I'm positioned between.

Look!

In this first, I'm a Forest Huntsman
between two Male Does.
In this second, I'm a Queen
between two Hawaiian Fishermen.
In this third, I'm a *Louche*
between two liquor bar strippers.
In this fourth, I'm a Candy Cardinal
between two Angel Prisoners.
We blaze in this mish-mash.
We are not separated.
We are festooned.

True Voice

I'm a guest
for 'Breakfast on the Patio'.
Views
are all in patches, woods to the lake,
to other woods across.

White clouds
are static in the water. There is another guest.
His eyes are blue.
The eyes of the hostess,
dark.

This other guest
is a singer.
He's found a new teacher
who lives on the longest island in this land.

This teacher is Austrian
and has hand-built a house with outside studio.
In this studio, he is teaching the singer
to be a tenor.
The teacher concentrates on *Lieder*.
He loves *Lieder* for its narrative arc.

Soprano birds
in the morning
use their primary head register,
but an element of *'get a load of this fellas'*
escapes from the warble in their throats.

Taking off from the lake,
sea planes
bound for Alaska
use their great hurt abdomen register.
As the planes get higher, the hurt is the sound in the chest
of crows.

After breakfast,
many birds in branches tangling.
A high branch

on a high tree
tangles not with anything

but waits for male contraltos,
any kind of alto,
late developing sopranos.
Horizontally it stands.

Background Music

1
After food, there was no money for clothes—
so Gran told me to wear the suit of my dead Uncle.
Days before the war's end his plane had crashed into poplars
as he'd been coming in to land.
                         Though big for 12,
I was too small for the vestments of a 23 year old martyr.
"Either you put it on or go starkers.
Do as you're told."

The light blue jacket of the light blue suit reached my knees
(in my family there was little stitching)
and the trouser bottoms were kept in a roll by elastic bands.
The Couzin children laughed at me outright.
And though the reasons for this not to matter
were that they were dirty (The Dirty Couzins) and had a Dad
who couldn't read—the regular staccato in their cackle
illustrated they were super sure of what they'd seen.

After this reaction in the nearby urban population,
I was morose. Ever notice how trees are not untidy,
however shrouded?
I was the wrong-sized shape.
I was an old callus
in a young universe
carrying a dead man's clothing,
covering a soul
unfinished—
quite complete.

2
Mind you, nature is full of ill will—
which descends as readily on those outfitted by tailors
as on those in hand-me-downs.
In London I have a lovely London friend
in one of those rectangular blocks called *Mansions*—
rectangular blocks enclosing gardens.
He has lost respect for religion, has tired of philosophy,

knows modern art is just a prank
and so concentrates on clothes.

One night wearing brand new silk pajamas, he's in bed
between laundered sheets, when he's woken
by a commotion from his front room
where a balcony over the main door entrance
means his second floor apartment
can be climbed up to from the road.

Commotion. As of burglars panicked, except no voices.
Commotion as of debutantes playing a game learnt at school
and the game in their head is not remembered in their toes.

A bloody huge magpie had come down the chimney—
unable to get out of the apartments on the floors overhead
(with fireplaces converted to the electrical)
it was thus enclosed.
My lovely London friend
opened the middle-of-the-night windows,
but the great black bird
extending itself on the back of the couch
was making itself at home. The longer it stayed,
the more apt the magpie. An apt magpie
in a sitting-room raises doubts in the beholder
who once had a flash of understanding
but is now befuddled in the muffled middle
of being treacherously human and not a bird.

Evident Bed

Eternity may not the chance repeat,
But I must tread my single way alone,
In sad rememberance that we once did meet,
And know that bliss irrevocably gone.

Henry David Thoreau

Love On The Roof

                On the evening of June 10th
                I go with a new friend to the movies.
                The film is about Sicilians
                getting to America.
                They have to cross the Atlantic
                in a ship that is falling apart.
They carry photos
of an American tree
growing coins in the branches.
Giant golden apples
coconuts pineapples pears.
                Intermittently
                they bathe in rivers.
                These Rivers are Empire Rivers
                with a milk white bright shine.
The new friend decides
I'm just too old
so he goes back to his apartment
and I have dinner alone.
My apartment looks south
to the Liberty Tower,
avocado asparagus brussel sprouts.
                I get out of bed
                at 5:45 the next morning.
                Passing through
                the living room
                on my way to make tea,
                I glance out
                at the overcast sky
and there's a naked
young woman
performing fellatio
on a naked young man
(well, he's wearing a blue T-shirt)
on the opposite roof.
                Someone clever once said:
                "Our eyeballs are evolved
                by the sun for the sun
                to be looked at!"
                              What??!!

                    A blow job is undeniably happening,
                    not contingent on me or my eyesight.
My eyesight
is not so good.
Yet they were as exposed as
the 'Princess' who sleeps on the bed
and feels the 'Pea'.
                    This has not the least relevance,
                    but I'm confused—
                    as in a light
                    not as solid as early night,
                    and not as light
                    as early summer bright,
                    I search for an analogy
                    to this naked surprise.
And it's to be out
with a new lover in a restaurant
telling him I'm getting into Proust.
                        "Proust takes analysis
                        beyond analysis.
                        Proust shows
                        the development
                        of masochism
                        in his love-lorn
                        protagonist."
My new lover
sitting in the restaurant says,
"Proust, I'll show you Proust! "
And opens up his fly.
                    I prepare tea in the dark morning.
                    To put on my light would disturb them.
                    I'm going to find my glasses in a minute
                    —where are my long range glasses? —
to find out
if anyone is watching them from the expensive
new apartments way across the way.
                          I'm not watching.
                          I'm making tea
                          inside my windows.
                          I have the right.
She stands and so does he.
Then in an exquisite moment
they bend over each other—

>   young humans
>   realizing
>   they'll never get the whole thing
>   of each other.
>   Accepting, like me,
>   that a part of the human plight
>   is to never get the whole
>   of the other
>   in plain view sight.

I don't think
the teaspoon tinkled
or the tea over-sprinkled—

>   yet, disturbed, they move
>   behind a water tower,
>   one of those blasted
>   New York City roof constructions.

In that direction
are more windows.
Are they fooled only because
these windows of rich apartments
are far enough to be farther away?

>   She's thin ungainly graceful
>   with enough self-possession
>   to retain composure

screaming 'Fire!'
after waking up in a strange bed.
I ascertain this with certainty
as she moves out of sight

>   and he stumbles after
>   with pants around his ankles,
>   showing something
>   to write home about,
>   for as he stumbles
>   his accoutrement sways.

Four cookies and tea
are taken to the bedroom
where I find my glasses.
Yes, they are long range.

>   My bed is up against the window.
>   And her blue leather handbag
>   and his backpack
>   with a camouflage pattern
>   are crucial details
>   of the rectangular world—

the world rectangle
made by the bottom of my window
and the raised six inches of my blind.
When they return
they are stark bollock naked.
They dress. And in his pants and T-shirt,
he looks smaller younger
with hands and face bronzed enough
                                        to be the color
                                        of the populace of
                                        the Peloponnesian village
                                        I once visited
                                        on a mistaken visit
                                        to a mistaken place.
She's stylish in black top and jeans.
Maybe she lives in the building.
He has a backpack, so lives far off.
They kiss goodbye.
They leave.
                And I'm stuck with this empty roof
                until young men stop wearing Adidas pants.
                They were Adidas.
                The three stripes were plain.

Missed Connections

If you are the business man
who gets on the Downtown 6 subway at Grand Central at 8:15
carrying a crocodile attaché

      your suits, the best synthetic, with invisible lines—

I am the older guy who sits next to the door
in grey woolen fabric with a lining of polyester
mixed with cotton. Polyester/cotton
is a temperature-control silken wonder.

      Often I open myself up to flash my sheen.

Not quite middle-aged, you are quite white
with an intelligence honed in Connecticut,
spanked into adulthood by a Step-Daddy who retired early.

      He retired to Maine.

Until he retired you had an office next to Daddy's.
"Benjamin! Can you see to this?"
Daddy's exclamations withstood many a recession.
                                        "—Benjamin!"
      His whine was a threat, his threat was a whine.

You always got hard as Daddy spanked
(with mother and wife out of the house).
At work employees followed the *slaps* in secret,
remembering similar urges

      in technical buildings with identical cries.

Daddy administered retribution with a paddle.
He cared nothing for justice, but adored correction.
Correction prevented your hardening
in the fashion of accountancy. Your face isn't disfigured

      with certainty: the financier's lie.

Step-Daddy, now in his 70's, doesn't come to New York.

For spanking sessions you go to Maine.
Daddy lives near the Canadian border.
After spanking you go over, over the border

        to a region rejected by cartographers. Away.

There are linings and linings. Linings to linings.
On weekends I bet there's a lining inside your jeans!
Before we know it,
you have to go on to Wall Street after my descent at 14th.
If you read this, send an Email to Jondollar@earthlink.net.
Benjamin! I love the light lovely lining

        against my forearms, inside my sleeves.

GONE WILD

After prison he takes it as given
he'll have no money no job no love.
So he becomes a tele-marketer.

He chooses his own hours and starts at dusk.
We all know what happens at dusk,
e.g. 'The park closes at dusk'.
So that is a plus—starting at dusk,
starting when the light is vanishing
and his voice can beam in from the dark.

"Are you the head of the household?
I'm conducting a survey
and I want to present you with an opportunity.
I have here *Girls Gone Wild*.
It's a DVD, and it's bad."

At the other end, silence
as the prospective client
sorts out—*How much are they male?*
How much, female?
To what are they attracted?
How much does class matter
and nipples and bollocks and ass?

Into this confusion he proffers,
"Also I have here a copy of *Boys Gone Wild*."
Thus he takes a jump
and is all sex to all creatures.
With a giggle then,
he activates their animal spirit—
and the realization there is comedy in it
makes possibilities wild.

In the middle of their laughter he jumps to the survey
which gives an air of legality.
"I have two questions.
Question one. Drama? Comedy? Adult?
Which is preferable? —Eh! What a good answer.
Question two is a political abstraction.

Hope I don't drain your brain.
Nothing wrong with watching *Girls Gone Wild*
or *Boys Gone Wild* in the privacy of your home?
—Yeh! Agreed!

It is eight dollars for each video separately
but you can have both for twelve.
Listen up.
Say you have a desire to view a patch of wild mountain heather,
you have to put your hand in your pocket
to pay for transportation —
and from the state of the planet you better get on with it.

Similarly,
the video market is past its zenith.
In a split second the Lord created the Spirit.
So, on the instantaneous combustible, remember—
the Lord never giveth back that what he hath taken away."

Street Scenes

In a restaurant near West 4th subway station
I'm having an after dinner drink
with a friend who translates poems from the Indian.

The crowd outside on 6th Avenue is surging
as if to break through the window,
into *our* canvas, the restaurant—
to get out of *their* canvas, the packed and colorful street.

As in any New York area there are smatterings of
larky charlatans,
politico politicos,
intentional unintentional beauties,
diplomatic democratic religions,
rip-roaring greed.

Into this turbulence
wanders a porno star
in love with fame,
the kind of youth to be seen cruising in graveyards
among the naked tombstones.
Actually I'd seen him in a car outside my building
the year before.
I'd wanted to say "Are you waiting for me?"
—because I'd been watching him on a porn site just previously.

In videos, he is *powerlessness*.
In the flesh, he's activity without commentary.
And when I saw him
I worshipped him,
though in his car I could only see a bit of him.
Now, on West 4th looking at the whole of him,
it's easy to submit.

A teenage Puerto Rican.
One of his best videos is *'Rico-Structions.'*
In it he plays an architect beset by construction workers.
Frustration resides in these construction workers.
His function is to recognize frustration, and commit.

I'd also seen him sitting in the F train,
but again just the upper part of him—
for I was standing on the platform
with sweat pouring off of me.
(That was a summer of great heat.)

I point out my porn star to my poet friend,
the translator from the Indian.
My friend sees a resemblance to figures on Indian temples.
"No," I correct.
"He's a hieroglyph on prehistoric monuments,
and his limbs are paragraphs
waiting to wrap round the warriors
of the bison hunting plains."

To corroborate I look to the street
but there's no sign of him now. I grieve.
My friend is humiliated.
"You're embarrassing.
I didn't know you were a pornographic Queen."
"I'm not...I just like to be powerfully teased.
Also I like the propulsion to be found in recent novels.
Now how are we going to pass the time?"

We watch the sexual athletes pass along 6th Avenue.
All pass beyond the frame of our consideration
to display themselves like ships on deep appreciative seas.

Looking for Bottoms

Two

top-of-the-list Bottoms
phoned
at the last moment
and said,
"We're going to be late."

I said,

"Take your talents
to a different planet.
Lack of professionalism
belongs outside the Milky Way."

So,

if you are a Bottom
and can travel to Astoria,
please apply.

If

your application is accepted
expect to be paid
at the end of the evening.
Remuneration is based
on a word-of-mouth contract.

Listen up.

The promise
is going to be emailed—
"You'll receive good remuneration.
Rest in peace."

Accepting

all and any colored bottoms,
to go along with multi-colored tops.

(An amount of shuffling is expected,
with an awareness that opposites attract.)

Therefore,

if you have a smooth bottom
social skills
good proportions
decent height
and have an enthusiasm
for promiscuity
yet can use yourself
monogamously

unconcerned

with definition
and enjoy
the primordial—
then email
a photo of your hot arse
with face.

Best

if the image
is no more than two years old.
I stress—dishonesty will *not* be tolerated.
Dishonesty disappoints.

The Tops

are virile African Americans,
macho Latinos,
and a few blue-collared fertile Whites
amongst whom I've discovered
a large number of Republicans.
A year ago I would have been surprised.

Let's be

open-minded
as well as being voracious.

There should be a quality of distance,
as in admiration of stained glass
in a French Cathedral
where grandeur
is on equal par with detail.
Don't be afraid of grandeur!
Don't be afraid of detail!—
More gratifying than size.

MASSEUR

If you are looking for *security*,
also known as s*afety*
aka, *certainty*—
let me introduce you to massage therapy
as practiced by my masseur.
He'll be in New York
until the third week of April.
If you need an appointment
make it immediately
because as soon as he advertises
his appointment book is full.

Once you've had one appointment
you'll want one after another
cos he's a top-notch,
high-end, highly infectious, disease free,
5 foot 11 inches of cute sanity.
A forty year old American white boy,
dark hazel eyes, 170 lbs, dyed blond hair.
Sessions are a combo of invigorating military
and Swedish deep tissue,
with a therapeutic detour
in high-grade unscented oil
dispensed from his personal table.

His creativity is mothered by scientific action.
Causing this old fart to behave like a tart,
fulsomely disintegrating/integrating—
I didn't half-laugh.
He'll be wearing knitted pants
delineating his parts,
in scented low lighting.
After pleasant chit-chat
you'll both get undressed
and human life will be more convivial
as he shows his torso to you
and you show your torso to him.
Such pleasure should not belong to the past;
such a scene rarely happens
and you pray it will last.

Soon you are being massaged
not with greasy amateur grease
but smooth odorless cream.
His strokes will move you
to the banks of rivers.
You'll stroll along the Nile
with the strut of King Tut,
the King who married his brother
(this masseur is your brother).
Anglophones can believe
they're the beloved Queen Mother
examining after-blitz damage
by the side of the Thames.

When his touch has totally confused you,
he'll pull out his *Kodak Z650*
with which he feels comfortable
and leave you with 40 to 50 quality poses
of a vivid *what is*—
forget the *might have been*.
His photography proves
our bodies express more than chaos,
so do not be frivolous.
Amphetamines, cocaine, pot,
do them previously—
no drugs in his space.
And please stay awake.
He won't work after eight.
He wants you to know
happiness exists not in the future, but now.
His massages are hourly,
half-hourly if you are short on cash.
But when hourly—he gets right on top of you,
he is the surfer and you are the sea
from the way he touches you.
Please
don't believe he's in love with you.
And never, never ask him to do you for free.

His premises are located
in an exceptional brownstone.
There's a map on his website,
www.tantriccomrade.com.

Surrounding ironwork will remind you of Europe,
possibly London—
though in European countries, because of war,
little ironwork remains.
The ironwork in Brooklyn is pure. Not an amalgam.
What is wrought in quality is deeply rooted,
not worn on the sleeve.

CRUISING

1

I'm sleeping
but a jangle jangles me.
It's the phone.
If it had been door and phone together—

BANG BANG BANG WENT THE DOOR KNOCK.
RING DING DING WENT THE PHONE.

—would one have protected me from the other, to some degree?
The man on the phone is my friend David.
As well as speaking, he's sobbing—

MONEY IS THE ROOT
OF ALL EVIL.

—David is rich.
At a party I'd sat down on a chair in his apartment
and guests had whispered "Get off that chair. It's museum worthy." —

A HOUSE
IS NOT A HOME.

—I can't recognize antiques.
His news is,
"I'm leaving at dawn on a cruise to the islands.
I'm offering you a spare ticket.
You'll have your own cabin. Your own cabin! Accept!"
What had happened was that David fell
hook line and sinker—

OH YOU BEAUTIFUL DOLL.
YOU GREAT BIG BEAUTIFUL DOLL.

—hook and line and sinker for the 25 year old waiter
in *The Lollipop Bar*.
The waiter moved in.
The waiter was ensconced.

The waiter, eyes astride,
drank Jack Daniels from David's cupboard
where other precious articles were locked.
Also, while David was out antiquing, the waiter entertained—

I'VE GOT A LOVELY BUNCH OF COCONUTS.
BIG ONES. SMALL ONES.

—entertained laborers, politicians,
entertained even Australians,
anyone so inclined.
David hired a private eye
and the waiter's behavior was discovered.
The transference of the ticket (to me)
was the end of their relationship, defined.
We reach Greece
and there's an end of the cruise party. But David—

SET EM UP JOE.
I'VE GOT A LITTLE STORY I WANT YOU TO KNOW.

—David stays in his cabin, plunged into drink.
I need a glimpse of the island.
Is it surrounded by water? Is it Greek?
I buy sunglasses at a stall on a bay
where the Persian fleet was scuttled by the Greeks
or the Greeks scuttled by the Persians.
And one of the Kings had sat on his throne
at the ring-a-ding edge of the lurid sea—

I DO LIKE TO BE
BESIDE THE SEASIDE.

—and that King died and David died and the waiter died
and the ship died and also me.

2
A billionaire, Mr. Money Bags,
asks me to go along on a luxury cruise.
In the middle of a recession,
he's raking it in.

BROTHER
CAN YOU SPARE A DIME?

The ticket he's given me is by rights his young lover's,
a 25 year old waiter from *The Lollipop Bar*.
But on the evening of departure
the lover's infidelities are unclothed:
infidelities committed with laborers in restricted areas,
entertainers in public conveniences,
politicians in dubious circumstances,
even an Australian in the middle of public lawns.

To ease his suffering
the billionaire convinces himself
to do something for the less fortunate.
I get the ticket
because I belong to the poorer classes—
and though younger than him, I'm old.

The cruise ship is perfection.
What's meant to be hot is hot.
What's served with ice is cold.

But the sea is full of fish that leap,
conjuring images of his young lad lover
leaping boundaries that are always covered.
As we float by Venice, the billionaire is deep into grief.
His anguish is unreachable opposite Greece.

HE'S DOWN AND TROUBLED
AND DOESN'T WANT A HELPING HAND.

When we visit an island
at the end of the Mediterranean,
Mr. Money Bags stays drunk in his cabin
while the tour-guide hands out maps on which she's written,
W's for *W*onderful
and *U*'s for *U*ninteresting.

We pass between the houses of a village
where large balconies stare at other balconies
across a dusty pathway,
and all is turned inward from countryside and sea.

On the map: *U* for *U*ninteresting. I don't agree.
If there was any concern for aesthetics,
the balconies would watch the Aegean.
But this village isn't concerned with the correct place proper.

I WAS DRIVING ACROSS THE BURNING DESERT
WHEN I SPOTTED SIX JET PLANES.

The balconies stare at each other across a weedy track
which isn't supposed to be a street.

Meeting

There was this encounter
a *meeting*
between me
(who I've come to know as a white guy from England)
and a black guy
(who turned out African American)
at 11AM
in the lower part of New York City
on April 2nd 2-zero-sixteen.
As he walked,
the black man kept his expensive coat with fur trimming open
to display—
an ambulance man's jacket?
a chef's short overall jacket?
a dental assistant's coverall jacket?
The white material, in passing, splashed
to meet attentions hidden away.

"Good Morning," he intoned.
I leaned because I am an old tower with weedy flowers,
with sprigs in bowers,
a night-scented stock.
Once he'd passed
it was easy to recognize there'd been the healing of a split,
a desire for desire,
a buzz.

"Good morning," he had said.
And I continued to the deli—
where before going in, I wondered,
sharp as an animal experiencing envy,
Good morning! What does he mean by that?
He'd stopped where there was nothing to stop for
in between blocks—
to the point where he was stationary!
So I walked back.
He was on his cell phone,
but the street was convinced he was speaking to nobody.
We'd both had experiences
but not this experience,

so don't know what to believe.
I came up with, "That is a great tie."
Indeed, right down his front,
the large tie supplied an answer to frustrations:
either black stripes on white, or white stripes on black,
it proved we have brains.
"Live near here?"
"Yeah," was my answer.
"Lead the way."

Straight talk

In a winter season
>under a hard sun
>I sit outside the senior building,
>dressed in the body of a senior citizen.

A turbaned Indian approaches.
>"I am a brick examiner,
>an engineer that prevents your building
>from falling.
>Forgive my asking, but are you still working?
>Nature has knitted you too young a face
>to be retired.

Oh!—an English teacher were you?
>We Indians speak in a fashion of translation
>as if to prove great authors must be Asian.
>Honored Professor, if you correct my usage—
>I'll do anything in return.
>Forgive my asking! Are you a gay?
>One who believes experience is erect?
>To me you appear that type of man.

I'm correct, if I'm not mistaken.
>One day you and I will have a try.
>Are you sexed on?
>Or is it you who sex?

Perhaps I'll love it.
>Give up work for it.
>Change is inevitable!
>That's how I'll explain it to my wife.
>Do you have children? No matter.
>You can be one of mine."

After this cross-cultural conversation,
>the senior building,
>high on joy
>rises to its full height.
>Then, when it leans in a dark slant,
>accoutrements of Indian culture

>   —Siva, a Sitar, the Gita—
>   fall from the roof . . . . CRASH SLIDE

Everything that is, is engineering
              up to and including conversations,
              celebrations of recurrent rituals,
              and the holding out of palms
              to test the bending of beliefs.

One
  Two
    Three

one
Two strangers see an Idea.
Hulking up.
Needn't be an Idea,
but a Think pumpedup.
So the Strangers grab each other
cos if they don't the Think will creep away,
sorry for itself.

    two
    They find themselves
    in a house one of them says is his
    at the end of New York City
    or the beginning of Long Island
    where they vaguely fool around.

        three
        Could we posit
        who's in charge?
        Is there a winner—
        with one more encouraged,
        the other more engaged?
        Orgasm is not the question
        (private explosion and defeat).
        On this beach
        spread-tides advance,
        wavelets retreat.

HOTEL

Xmas Eve
        embroiled with a hustler in midtown,
he suggests an escape. The hotel
is at the end of 42nd street
                the only one remaining where clients pay
                thirty bucks for a two-hour stay.

42nd street
        is bright bright bright
and satiated with electric anonymity.
We seek religious preparation
for tomorrow's holy day. Outside
                the harsh commercial,
                  we'll find our different way to pray.

The three story hotel
                says *Seasonal Greetings* in waning neon,
concordant with an exterior painted diluted lemon
for the sake of taste being squeezed. Behind
                street level glass doors
                fourteen steps lead to more glass doors.
                Long ago it was too late to reconsider.

This was realized
                when ancestors used sea-lorn tentacles,
when Chaucer chose who was going to Canterbury
based on the religious sexuality of the Crusades.
All doors are open. The female custodian
                with the seriousness
                of a South American pope
                leads the way.

Evident bed
        has been evidently waiting.
Similar to a visit at an altar,
we don't need a key. No decoration
                sheets quilt walls sink faucets
                are cleaner,
                the room as plain as the manger
                where a ritual was forged
                by Three Kings.

Once
    the door is shut
the room supports transgression, transfiguration—
which is the job of rooms on Xmas Eve. Uptown
              mansions with open curtains
              exhibit the extravagance
              of expensive shadows
              made manifest in shapes.

Decorous
    lighted downtown windows
celebrate the sexless birth
that led to change. Intuition
              tells us when two hours are up,
              when the inclinations of 42nd street
              will be sacredly appeased.

How hard to understand,
difficult, hard,
obscene, vague, indistinct,
this morning of so much light
with afternoon full on us,
treading water till night takes ours.

JOHN ASHBERY

To Walk The Walk

Generally on Saturdays we go to the movies.
Parker comes round at 5pm and we pick cinema and film.
But last Saturday was warm—
so we decided our lives should be out and about,
and to discover what might be on the agenda
we went for a walk.

On Delancey Street a vendor
(Danish Haitian? Icelandic Sicilian?)
was shaving ice from a block.
He heaped the ice in a paper cup
and when he poured on blueberry syrup we wanted to lick him
for creating purply patterns to be savored and gulped.

He tried to sell us a variety called *Rainbow*,
but it resided in a clean steel container ready to be scooped.
We insisted on the ice and syrup,
so he filled our cups with the shaved ice—
on Parker's he poured violent strawberry
the color of the wounds on an extraordinary body,
on mine he poured calming coconut.

This vendor belongs to an ancient tribe.
In New York City they work on food carts,
in restaurants, and in bars.
Gender-wise they are both Ulysses and Penelope.
Ulysses and Penelope meet in our ice,
flirt in our esophagi, in our stomachs perform loving rights.

After Delancey Street we cross the pedestrian bridge
to the East River.
Beneath our feet roars the FDR with swift motorized citizens,
all cursed with complete concentration on destination.
And us too. For the East River is our weekend ambition,
our troublesome need.

In East River Park, an ancient Latino
noticing I am white and Parker black,
asks, "How y'all doing, you old Peppers and Salts?"
Stretched leisure is the time within his question.

Time made up of long moments.
Also, the facts in his question don't attack.

Under the Williamsburg Bridge
a Chinese fisherman has caught a fish.
In the shallow water of a green bucket the silver fish wonders,
"If I try harder, will I live?"
Parker, and I, and the fish
open our wide fish eyes
to get a hook in the situation.

It's ungraspable, uncatchable,
but we try.

River

'A mother, son, daughter and daughter's husband
walk down the slope of the village
to celebrate the son's 15th birthday on the river banks.
What a morning! Ordinary and extraordinary.
The earth surges and the sky shows off clouds
which are its pets.

The mother is a cook in the new canteen of the village school.
With the war over, 'hunger' is less part of a kids' vocabulary.
Food is still rationed
but gravy and meat and cheese are no longer an event.

The son-in-law has a high position in the nearby town's asylum.
He believes insanity is the result of a lack of privacy.
During the war 'to connect' was a mandate.
Post-war society needs a commitment to the secret life.

The daughter works behind the counter in the town post office.
A survey is taking place
so all transactions are ticked off in a numbered space.
Two experts, hired to oversee the survey,
behave as if personal efficiency is/was
the aim of the war that raged.

The fifteen year old son is a beauty,
in a stage of puberty which knows
railway bridges across rivers
dream of being made love to by pitiless trains.
In sleep he's cursed with sweet orgasm, often.
His mother is disgruntled from having to wash the sheets.

At the river the son gets into his swimsuit immediately.
And while showing mother-sister-brother-in-law
his new swimming ability,
is pulled by the current into a whirlpool.
Next day his body is retrieved.
As he is sucked under what presents itself
as a calm stretch of water,
his thoughts are—"Mam, I can't. My eyes will be pearls.
Oh, please."

When the family returns up through the village,
they can't tell the difference between the surfaces of water
and the clarity that is the day.
When will they get back to working?
All have important jobs. Especially the mother.
Part of democratic services, she's expected to be cooking.
The government has provided a white overall.
And if she doesn't work, she won't get paid.

Naked Nudes

To reach the nudist beach
we get to Mykonos port really early.
The small fishing boat is overloaded,
and the suspicious sea
has a surly shine.
Coffee stall with coffee plaza
looks down into the nudist area.
A lot can't wait to drop their knickers,
to rush where
breast is titties
dick is dickies
ass is bums.
Among those remaining—
overclothes, underclothes,
one by one discarded,
until a group around a table
never ready for an occasion
wonders:
What's happiness got to do with this?

I'm last to peel off my beach shorts.
Anxious for the covering of the sea, I fly down the sand
with no stops on my roadway.
The island's voice narrates:
You are a piece of machinery
with an unstoppable gait.
Yet
I buckle double as I enter the Aegean,
for below the surface are sharp small rocks.
A figure runs to get first aid equipment—
its bollocks lollop, its body hair whistles,
as it returns with a box
containing
ointments for feet with gashes and cuts.

But what is in question
on the day of my feet's mutilation
is a Greek at the edge of the Aegean
wearing only a jacket and leading a donkey.
Both he and the donkey

have sturdy expressions and stout dicks.
No sign of a dwelling!
Did the idea of wearing
the dark jacket come from the depths of his brain,
or a more physical place?

He and the donkey as statuary—
forever along the line where sea hits the beach,
the dark jacket persisting into the distance.
A dark jacket with a donkey,
out walking,
in juxtaposition to hundreds of nudists,
all getting into a pose
to be viewed deferentially,
lest Greek and donkey see them
as a profusion of organs bounded by skin.

Peace

(ON THE BUS, 1946)

After the Second World War,
in a period given the name of *Peace*,
a new fashion of activity was floating.

During the war buses had been a long time coming;
but this bus, journeying to the market,
had arrived when it was supposed to

and this 'on-time' service
was as taken-for-granted now as the Sun
which would be there when I next saw it.

Well it would be, wouldn't it?
                              —Be again?

Also the wood-slatted seats had changed
to a newly discovered 'upholstery'—
animal-colored, rectangular squares

bordering the smell of my uncle.
Then, as I admired the ex-soldier's hand
at the end of the arm of my uncle,

the bus jerked. It's kind of amazing
when the complex energy of an accident results
in a jolt—the beginning of one chapter, the end of another.

For further along the road a man had been hurt.
This news was relayed over the stalled traffic
from where the accident had marooned him.

A worker, he'd been crushed by a lorry.
He'd been pouring concrete—
creating, out of the floor and walls of a dribbly brook,

an irrigation canal.
One of his legs had been severed.
And his wife, on our bus, had expected to wave

to him, while passing to the market—
to the complete him,
while passing to the market in the town.

She was wearing a felt hat, for in this period of *Peace*
women had stopped wearing scarves.
A brown circular hat with a pin in the crown.

With ne'er a sigh she was cradled along
from the back of the bus—
handed outside, carefully down.

And then with barely a wince
she was handed back
(for the ambulance had already collected her husband)

to re-inflate what had been flattened
in this period of nonviolence—
to re-construct what had been ground.

BICYCLE THIEF

As narratives go
there's little to compare
with the story of Tony,
an old guy who is going to die
and has a bike.
Pedaling to the supermarket
he passes Gil,
a younger guy also on a bike.
This young Gil
has an eternal animal look,
and Gil's bike and Antony's bike
fall for each other—
spoke for saddle,
saddle for spoke.

Tony's is stripped down expensive,
exposed wire, exposed desire.
Gil's is feminine, globular
with metallic ambition and lure.
With erotic pressure on the pedals
the wheel spokes disappear,
and through the four airy rotundas
are diligent landscapes
with spheres of lolloping bollocks
and Tony's funeral scene.

In the supermarket parking lot,
there's just one station left for parking bikes.
The eternal animal, Gil,
gets there before Tony, the guy about to die.
(This eternal animal Gil
is still alive today.)
Gil offers to surrender his parking rights—
"You got here first," he lies
through his set of American teeth.
"Please," Tony insists,
"there's room for your bike *and* mine."

Gil secures his 1960's mountain bike.
Though he may as well have left it unlocked,

for his lock is cheap.
Tony shows Gil his expensive lock
and there follows a discussion
of U-and-D locks.
Tony makes a promise,
out it comes, uncontrolled like a cough,
"I'll buy you a decent lock."
"I'm happy with what I've got," Gil replies.

They enter the supermarket
wondering if their bikes' emotional connection
has unified the roof of the shop
with the geometry of the sky.
Indeed the store has assumed a monastic quietude—
for outside, Tony and Gil's bikes are touching.
But as the clerks let out the moans of magnificent monks,
the roof blows off
because a thief, attempting to steal,
throws their two bikes to the ground

and wheels
pumps
handlebars
metal in general
in irredeemable orgasm
intertwine.

Lost Poem

The Beginning

A Drug Dealer's eyes come out of the dark.
Along with weed, he never fails to hand over his glance.

As he hands over marijuana in the shadows of a doorway
his sleek hair stretches back into a febrile bunch.

And always these glances. How many? Three? Four? Fifty?
In the dime bag the extraordinary weed is the color of bark.

Before it can be ascertained if his glances only belong on the periphery,
a bullet smashes through his skull. From front to back.

Territorial problems? Testosterone inadequacy?
Romantic jealousies? Debt? Certainties sprout.

Clients, family, friends bring extravagant flowers
to the lamppost where he was shot.

And I write a poem about different ways of dying.
A year later an editor says—

"I'd like to publish your poem
about the Latino with hair squeezed back."

But I'd lost the exercise book I write in. Anyway,
I'd transferred the poem to a computer, and the computer crashed.

My poem concerned drinking a cup of coffee
when I went into the street the morning after.

I'd drained my cup as police ribbons fluttered—
and death remained death, whatever I drank.

The End

To resurrect my poem I visited the funeral home
where they'd held the wake.
I'd tried to visit at the time of his murder
but the line had been around the block.

Today there is a line for another murder, but the line is short.
The body in the coffin is quite unlike my dealer.

My dealer was a tall guy who wore leather.
Instead of lank low pants, he wore loose jeans hitched up.

A Mafia *wanna-be* introduces himself to the room
as the 'Angel of Vengeance'.

He's going to search for the perpetrator
cos the law does *diddly-diddly-squat*.

A nun sings *Amazing Grace*, accompanying herself at the piano.
Her faith will never unravel. It's tied in a hard religious knot.

I'm accepted as a possible anthropologist
working for *National Geographic*.

The upholstered chairs with overstuffed cushions
suffocate emotions.

Unfairness is the wilting of the funeral flowers.
Wilting flowers absorb the sobs.

Flood

It's easy to forget (damn! I could finish the poem here).
It's easy to forget Manhattan is an island.
A way to remember is to hop on the Circle Line,
on to a boat as large as a department store—

and while circling the island,
buy an understanding of the city as a body
with water smash-lashing its prominent parts,
its private piers.

The voyage begins on the river at far West 42nd Street.
Over a superior system
a guide's voice delivers news
dictated by the arrangement of waters, of primal tides.

There is some doubt about
our squeeze around the top of Manhattan.
*"If at 96th Street the tide has risen too high
to pass under the bridges*

the boat will turn back in the direction it came from."
We'll still be thriving,
still be jiving,
but in reverse.

Thus is broken the promise
that the boat will circumnavigate
the island
(a natural system).

Ladies and Gentlemen won't have the opportunity
of playing Sir Francis Drake
with cod-piece
bringing about circular effects in the obscene seen world.

Passengers are disconsolate.
Particularly a Welsh poet
who under conventional clothing is wearing
lingerie with lace all around—

wearing meticulous lace
to experience shivering lacy freedom—
and hoping,
after a difficult squeeze around the top of Manhattan,

to exit the East River
and come out on The Hudson
filled with the ease
of Henrietta Hudson Galore.

Other star passengers,
Texan daughters
with incestuous fathers,
Persian transsexuals with a feel for temples,

musicians who never touch their instruments,
Libertarian Ethiopians—
all fall into a paroxysm
about the uncertainty of the known.

As the boat sails south along the West Side,
the guide points out prisms,
rectangular altars,
religious cones.

The city has been transformed!
Instead of drug-sleazed sex at the dark tops of buildings,
Rock Idols maintain surreal apartments
where stars come out to be revered.

When the 96th Street Bridge appears almost submerged
and nobody does nothing—
as the boat turns,
the guide keeps yapping.

Movement of Oceans
dictated by the inconstant moon
is inconsistent.
However—

liquid is known
to change its nature
Tides will reverse,
defenses will hold.

Brooklyn Bridge is nearly under.
A seagull's screech is lightning frightened by the thunder.
And in a dingy, over where Brooklyn Ferry used to be,
sits Whitman's ghost.

We'll all be let off at the Statue of Liberty.
Them with a ticket
will be allowed up the staircase.
They'll sit in the crown because they've reserved.

EARTHQUAKE

I was sitting at my table having lunch when
—*EH! SOMETHING WAS ON THE SPIN*—
beyond ethics
untroubled by understanding
beyond chaos
unconcerned with gravity
up
or down.
(Or is consciousness without, within?)
Whether it was the yearning of the Americas evolving
or a heart attack
or a stroke from too much wanking—
no way to tell!

How was I to know this was an earthquake,
with its center in Virginia,
torturing the rock below New York City,
indeed as far as Canada?
For this rock
according to experts
is a tremendous transmitter
and the quake was 5 point 9 on the Richter—
which is strong!

A painting an ex-boyfriend painted
of the Arizona desert when he was in Arizona—
shakes
leers forward
attempting a dance of adolescence
though it was painted 40 years before.
Poor thing doesn't have the flexibility of adolescence
or the stamina of a person in their twenties
or their thirties
or their forties
and so settles back
against the wall.

The tilted frame now renders the Arizona desert unsatisfied,
an unsatisfied place.
'*I CAN'T GET NO SATISFACTION.*'

When Mick was in his prime
and could get no satisfaction,
it wasn't a fact that came from an under-the-earth attack.
Everybody knew!

Nudes On Brighton Beach

London is as placid as expected
until my host suggests, "A visit to Brighton
might be a blast!"

On a website
devoted to nudism,
he's found at the edge of the sea
(where I'd expect it to be)
a nudist beach.

Brighton
is a town on England's south coast
with a long Victorian Pier.
There is an eccentric palace built by the Prince Regent.
Laurence Olivier,
in aged boned frailness,
lived here.

In this place of Regency elegance and Victorian decadence,
sea salt insinuates the fibers that clothe us—
and as far as we can taste,
our subconscious
is as amenable as Cotton Candy, as lickable as Fancy Nancy,
as Frolicsome as Rough Trade.

But the clock down the road from Brighton station yells,
in full frontal, "Past ten going on eleven!"
And with the prick of its everlasting tick adds,
"*Nothing* lasts—it all fades."

It is summer grey, and all is hilly.
Regency terraces stand at hilly angles to the hilly streets.
There are cozy cafes with the English classes—
Working, Middle, High, and Pure & Sweet.

Searching for what is lurking,
we come upon the English Channel.
From the Promenade we watch waves finish their journey.
Sea and land are concordant.
Concordant is not the same as neat.

To the left, the beach becomes stone and pebble.
Behind us, Brighton transforms into tracing,
neither in color, nor in black and white.

Lying in a puddle, a dead fish flashes an eyeball,
winking this essential information:
"Along this coast is Matthew Arnold's *Dover Beach*."

The nudist beach is rocks with nudists—
apotheosis of the horizon, apotheosis of the sea.
In foreground there are maybe twenty
mams/dads/sisters/brothers/cousins/lovers
in groups of two and three.

Their color is the color of those
who have taken their bodies out into the coldest.
They have the form of rocks, sods,
freedom of grass in swamps, courage of buds in difficult terrain.

Half a mile beyond on the high cliff edge, among parked cars,
a crowd is jostling
with binoculars, telescopes, phones, cameras.
The cliff is crumbling under blatant shapes.

Ah Love, let us be true to one another.
Let us squat by the English Channel,
which is the sea at Brighton,
ignore this crumbling, bound to happen,
live a definition of our own peace.

Tattoos

At a poetry reading
a straight African American recites...

> *Catholicism is great. Take a gander at its robe.*
> *A robin's breast like a cardinal's chest is theatrical and bold.*

Oh!
I want to stroke his exuberance,
bend his boundaries,
shave his head.

My Companion says,
"You can get along without him!"
My Queer White companion has glorious tattoos.

> *tattat TAT   tattat TAT tattat TAT ooooos*

This companion expounds:
my enthusiasm for the black poet
exposes a dissatisfaction with my own imagination—
my own odor, my color, my nature, my own clothes.

> *tattat TAT   tattat TAT tattat TAT clooothes*

Time passes
and death is lurking.
And at an interminable reading
an Activist Female states

> *Moaning copulation produces an agonzied population.*

Oh! She's lovely!
I want to be subjugated by her influences,
covet her woes.

> *tattat TAT   tattat TAT tattat TAT woooooes*

The Straight/Black poet,
now my lover,
whispers, "She designs her poetry for expensive bars."

Anyway, me and this female
become an item
influenced by symbolism,
so we pay attention when my white tattooed ex
appears at a reading with a very short poem.

> *Between my tattoos are areas quite unmarked.*
> *Between configurations I have avoided scars.*

My female activist instructs,
"Stop looking! All the bar knows what's cooking.
What do you see in him?"

"The rightful word."

Oh! I hope we get back together.
Ain't gonna be easy.
It's gonna be absurd.

Jail Or Rehab

        For longer than I can't remember
        I've been an addict.
        To cover my wounds
        my addiction has been bandaged.

From too much ointment
my bandage has slipped off totally.
Now—sex beer weed could cause a stroke.
Coke might render me quite blind.

        A situation has arrived
        where I'm offered jail or rehab.
        I choose rehab
        and walk through the facility—
        out into a troubled suburban pasture
        to cruise a stag.

Take a gander at his antlers!
Like his haunches, they're in mint condition!
But—I'm here to be pure.
Instead of buggery, I'll walk

        to a van, to be driven
        220 miles to a mansion in a rural setting,
        four beds to a room
        with a staccato radio blaring—
        this is the land where you belong.

Belong! Belong!—With its sound of a gong,
it's a song of not being anywhere.
So, in a foxy toxin of being too much somewhere,
I disappear on a country walk.

        There, in the forest,
        I meet a bear who gnaws.
        Wonderful to watch
        as his rough tongue talks—
        "I'm straight. You're gonna have to wait.
        We're gonna do it in the dusky middle
        of the befuddled dark."

To ascertain instability,
twice a week I'm returned to the city.
To get to the highway
we negotiate serpentine hillocks
on a gentle route with a steep grade.

        If I follow the rules
        an apartment will be found
        with extra for furniture.
        I'd prefer no furniture,
        with a door that gives onto a boardwalk.

Over the rail
a stillness, reminiscent of an operatic ocean—
I believe it's the Atlantic,
Flat Placid.
From Flat Placid waters will issue
the shocked bodies of the Liquid Dancers.

        They'll raise themselves up
        on transparent scales
        at the ends of their tails
        and sing through
        the grind of their teeth,
        "Do you have faith?"
        "—Well, I do have two empty rooms."

Back in the apartment we'll strip quite starkers.
And when we snuggle under the covers they'll call me Dad.
Their sea-weed hair smells of astonished bulbs.
Their eyes are packed with lightning—
forget about thunder
when flash after flash smiles its exasperated pain.

THE FULL SKETCH

    I never found them again
    — those quite haphazardly acquired,
    that I give up so lightly,
    and that later in aging I craved.
    The poetic eyes, the pallid face,
    I never found those lips again.

CONSTANTINE CAVAFY

Jock Doc

1.
I have skin cancer.
A bump of a lump is burnt or smoked out
by a much talked about doctor,
a sharp lesbian from the former French Guinea.
I ask her directly, "Where do you come from?"
"Guess!"
"I'd say Guinea."
"Wrong! I'm from The Sudan."

The bump of a lump was equidistant between my nipples
and my high point of gravity.
With a high point of gravity I have the courage to write poetry.
If the center of my being was a low point of gravity,
I'd be flattened flat in a permanent *lie-me-down-low*.

2.
Then a loop-shaped growth on the left back shoulder
is scooped out by a dermatologist youth.
When the cancer comes out wholesale he lets out a *whoop*.
He's scooped out the growth like a peach from a can.

This dermatologist is Lebanese.
He tells me, "Lebanon was originally Phoenicia.
Before the civil war, Lebanese men would go to the beach
and change into swimwear designed by Pierre Cardin."

This was in answer to my question,
"Was Lebanon once called *The Leban*?"

3.
A cancer is then discovered on my right nostril.
This cancer won't metastasize
(ie. attach itself to other organs)
but will get bigger then bigger then afterwards bigger.
Out it must come.

24 hours after the procedure,

I return to the hospital where a Jock of a Doc
(the plastic surgeon who did the op)
attacks my bandages, peels them off.
He is a Greek with roots in Sparta.
I'd ask him, "Where is Sparta?"—
but I already know about Sparta and its perverse goings on.

Then he shows a photo of me taken the day before,
unconscious on the operating table.
He had ferreted out the cancer
and the created hole is larger than the photo.
My body, up in a corner, is distantly Welsh.
The Welsh have a propensity for sitting at a window
wearing a cardigan,
watching moving forms move on.

4.
After I had the stroke
I couldn't remember my social security number.
A doctor and five or six nurses needed the answer right away.
I've had similar experiences
when I don't understand what is happening—
usually while I'm travelling.
On my way to Greece
I passed through Italy
where I'd forgotten Italian,
yet in a Yugoslavian bar
I ask for *un bicchiere di latte per favore*.
If you come from the British Isles this means, "I wonder
if by any chance you would be so kind as to sell me a glass of milk?"
A lot of this was happening as a result of the landscape
through which I was passing.
By the time I got to Athens *un bicchiere di latte* was forgotten.

When I finally got to the islands
I didn't have time for anything
cos Zeus did swoop.

Angry Romanian Surgeon

An article
   in my computer document file
      titled *Angry Romanian Surgeon*
         (sent by a English friend
           with a taste for perversity)
              remained unread.
                 I opened it up to get rid of it—
                    but at emotional expense.

I read:
   an Angry Romanian doctor
      cut off a patient's penis during surgery.
         Patient's name was 'Nelu'
           and surgeon's name was 'Naum'.
              Naum sliced off Nelu's pride and joy with a scalpel.
              Then, with bruised concentration,
                 placed it on an adjoining operating table.
                    Naum told the judge he'd lost his temper
                 as he was operating
               on Nelu's urinary channel.
               The judge, commiserating
                 with a surgeon's stress,
                   empathized with Naum.

I've never met
   a Romanian though I worked briefly for a Bulgarian,
      an ex-tennis champion with an art gallery
         near the Metropolitan Museum.
           I sat in his gallery, and made bids for him at auctions
              when he was at the Hamptons in his summer home.
              I sat in the middle of his specialization—
                 (mid-nineteenth century still lives,
                   usually flowers).
                    The genre was popular in the eighties.
                    The paintings were expertly effectual.
                    The dealers were elitist,
                       cut-throat-strong.

One weekend,
   an old woman snake-dancer enters with photographs.

She was living in New Jersey, in a home.
   She shows photos of herself
      with Boa Constrictor wrapped round.
      Would we show them in our gallery?
         (The Boa Constrictor died
            when he fell out the window.
               She'd lived on the 15th floor,
                  and the Boa Constrictor had loved the view.)

The porter
   tells the gallery owner of the snake-dancer's visit.
      The Bulgarian ex-tennis star
         turned nineteenth century aesthete
            asks what I'd done with an old woman
               in his gallery one warm afternoon.
                  "Photographs of her snake-dancing
                     are worthy of some national collection."
                        But there is to be no rationalizing.
                           "This is exactly the kind of woman
                              that can ruin a gallery's reputation."
                                 The visit of the snake-dancing woman
                                    causes turmoil
                                       in the short reaches
                                          of his limited concentration.

For permitting
   a snake-dancer of no visible means to relax amid his flowers
      the Bulgarian wants to do to me
         what Nelu had had done to him by Naum.
            As Nelu's parts had been placed
               on an operating table—
                  if I remain in the employ of this Bulgarian
                     my parts will be splayed across
                        the gallery's Italian mosaic floor.

The Bulgarian
   will quickly clean up the mess.
      For situated just off Museum mile
         who knows what art lovers might chance to come in.
            Art lovers have to have churned violence framed,
               producing a smooth mood
                  redolent of the Hamptons, Park Avenue, etc ...
                     all expensive homes.

Bank Manager

Our bank is a transparent battleship—
though nobody believes
'what you see is what you get.'
Bank Manager and Bank Employees and Bank Customers
(them what inhabit the battleship)
exemplify the purity
that surrounds atomic tests.

The manager,
blond extraordinary object among extraordinary objects,
is interviewing applicants for important positions.
Masculine applicants preen their packages,
competing with the packages of feminine applicants.
Packages are the hefted hammers
permitting professionals
access to the celestial granary.
And all's alright for the talented endowed.

After this display, both males and females
cross their legs to hide the sharp teeth of their Spirit.
In a bank, excess of spirit has the capacity to alarm.
Which doesn't prevent our manager, on the top floor,
from deliriously charming the digitized customers—
and, lower down, sexing the ATMs.
The bank is glass,
so his leaving of one space to enter another,
his greeting *and* leaving,
have the clarity of a burlesque arcade in a seaside town.

If such clarity makes you dizzy,
stand with your back to the bank
to watch the proceedings
reflected in the windows across the street.
The images are muddied,
but the bank manager's recognizable
in the fashion of personages
reflected in the utensils found in psychiatric suites.

Then, in a propitious hour,
the manager appears

over-clothed in 90 degree weather.
He has jumped out of the reflected image
and leads bank workers and clients
to Coney Island on the train.
Floating in the water he points out
that the horizon is a concoction—
like addition and subtraction.
Pleasure is leisure experienced in pain.

Unemployed In Philly

1.
ANOTHER WORKLESS MONDAY

Jason's coffee and toast have no personality.
This breakfast is as bland as Independence Hall
without a history. As suspicious as
government buildings without their stone.

                         Are his work mates still living?

Marc, his buddy, who worked with him in security?
The girl at the desk, her name 'Girl At The Desk'?
Does his boss retain that spiky expression
when watching TV alone?

                         This umpteenth Monday

he wanders like an Opera singer
never hired for Opera,
knowledgeable of texts and music
he'll never get to perform.

                         His Monday wife is still asleep

as are his sons of 5 and 7
who share a bed in the smallest room.
Worthless Mondays!

                         How many?

Jason sits on the edge
of his children's bed in his children's room.
Wife and children will believe
Jason left for work before Philly awoke,
got into the car before God spoke,
before night cracked into day, as day moved to the other coast.
Wife and children sleep

                         as Jason leaves.

Jason, no longer able to provide for his family,
drives out of the city over the bridge named *Benjamin Franklin*.
Then Jason drives back into the city
back over that same bridge
driving towards Philly in the nether direction
from which he'd decisively gone

                      after a round turn

back out of Philly.
The bridge is pensive with *Ben*'s philosophies,
with cables reputedly thick enough, supportive, strong.

                      Another round turn,

return into Philly,
never to be an element
in eighteenth century electricity,
never to be a revolutionary.
Jason returns to the apartment at 9.30.
Today his wife is undergoing chemotherapy,
the kids have left for school.
Monday morning will soon be gone.

2.
IN THE MIDDLE MORNING OF THIS MONDAY

From the apartment in the old city
he looks onto an elegant Quaker Meeting House,
a Meeting House erected to be never looked at
by a jobless married man.

                      Along a proportioned path,

an extravagant couple walks a dog.
They and their dog
buy their clothes expensively.
They match the Quaker house
in sublimity,
in the casing of a mood,
in an elegant pop song.

             Jason opens the window

and yells— "Cut out that barking! This is a silent zone!"
The man wants to know what is wrong
with the bark of an American
within the Meeting House grounds.

             Jason yells,

"I'm the Custodian,
the shoveler of the shit
amassed on these virtuous lawns."
"—And what are we?
Custodians of your Dissatisfactions?"

                    mouths the woman.

Her dog's stilettos
and her husband's 'built-ups'
manipulate the cobblestones
the three of them affronted.
"To be ordered about by a common o' gardener
is the worst of all possible wrongs!"

The Full Sketch

Zoe herself
is a work in progress,
so she follows her master
instantaneously
creatively
from the car
to the festival
in the town center
where
humans lean against storefronts
looking
at the carnival procession
over
the heads of other humans
on
the edge of the sidewalk
sitting
in holiday chairs.

Zoe
doesn't bark.
Her master
might think it unethical.
Instead she listens
to general criticism,
to criticism in general.

The crowd
thinks the Chinese
dreadful,
everybody's *awful*,
and

Poles Puerto-Ricans Mexicans
even couldn't
couldn't even
can't
keep in step.

Then humans on the sidewalk

part.
Those in chairs
move.
And as they make way for a thin figure
dressed
in what is meant to be
more or less, less or more, a bathing suit—
they whisper,
"Whore."

The whore
looks down to
Zoe,
Zoe
looks up
at whoredom—
another work in progress,
a full sketch.

"Whore. Whore."
It has a trumpety-trump of a sound—like *Prophet*.
This prophetic whore
enters the temple of condolence.
A bar.

And Zoe follows her master
to where
they'd been going—
the beach,
by means of car.
The visit to the festival
will never be forgotten.
Accidents
happen
year to month to week to day to hour to minute to second
and less
and more.

Zoe
relishes her job of belonging.
Never forgets
her male and female part,
her kids.

Let free
she runs down the flaunted stretch of sand
to the sea's edge and sees
whale,
a work in progress—
with gaze full on her,
vestured in the vigor
which supplies volition to the flesh.

Zoe senses her master
wants to come in with a bit of poetry:

> "*The whale*
> *returns to where its genes say it should be.*
> *And the broken water returns to Seadom.*
> *Seadom.*
> *The full sketch.*"

Nouns Must Go

Hey! The Ancient Puerto Rican
in the opposite apartment,
The Puerto Rican Ancient
wearing a short-sleeved summer shirt
in an unreasonable season,

the Rican Ancient, ogling shapes,
suffering from Alzheimer's, an Alzheimic Ancient—
he wandered out of the building in the depths of this morning
and his whereabouts remain unknown.

6AM, his grandson came directly from the night-shift
to look in on him, but didn't find him.
At 6:15 his home attendant arrived and phoned her agency
to say the Puerto Rican had again absconded.
He'd done it once before

and was discovered in the food market,
astounded by the multitudinous packs of cereal ascending,
and scared of the dead fish—
mingled, layered, and spread.

This is the miracle of dead fish flesh—
it's as vivacious as it ever was while swimming.
Free from the atrocious gesture appropriate to surviving,
the fish glistens, the counter flows.

The grandson and the home attendant
sit in the living room of the one bedroom,
just chairs and a table,
an Alzheimer Haven

—though the Rican was never bothered,
he couldn't tell the difference between a couch and a window,
pain from a children's playground,
the crooked from the raw.

According to the Alzheimic Authorities:
"Nouns are the first to go."
Taking a rest from the discombobulation of always being right,

nouns pack their belongings
and spend their days in a retirement home.

When this Ancient and I were both intact
we believed our *nouns* were actual facts.
Watching my apartment through the peep-hole in his door,
the Ancient saw PERVERTS and QUEERS
and DEMOCRATS and DYKES.

And watching his apartment through my peephole I saw
REDNECKS and HETEROS
and CATHOLICS and REPUBLICANS,
all there, to violate my magnificent personality,
to dismantle my monstrous faith.

Last week me and the Puerto Rican,
we waited for the elevator—two Ancients on a disparate voyage.
(We're talking on the ground floor wanting up,
not the top floor desiring down.)

On the way up I intended to ignore him:
to scrawl and crash and stamp
and break down the walls of the elevator,
and to rush into the discovered open space

so that me and the Puerto Rican
would never belong one to another.
I was designed to be a single man.
But the Alzeimic Ancient gazed and gazed—until
in the blank total of non-recognition

all elevations and extremities joined,
and drawn and magnetized together, we jigged a jig
that defied the limits of our disconnection.

With hands on what felt like the remnants
of each other's waists,
and looking into what had to be
the ruins of each other's faces,
we jigged a waltz, not fixed in space.

BOY'S WAR

The Second World War
is a boy's war.
      The boy lies in bed

to listen to the sound of war—
i.e. spuds in the garden expecting peace.
      When they are devoured others will take their place.

Listening to vegetation teaches him
the fall of leaves,
      breeds warmth into the cold of grief.

His father's Dad has four thumbs.
He's just learnt to count to 12
      and recounts, recounts, 12 digits on Grandad's hands.

The old man has a greeting:
"Look who's here!"
      when the boy comes visiting.

"Look who's here!"
Eight... nine... ten... eleven... twelve...
      Granddad's extra digits scare the boy then make him proud.

Dad and all men on battlefields abroad
go to make a thin home mix,
      mixed muddy by village functionaries where he lives.

The vicar, with a moustache related to Adolph Hitler's, brays:
"Our brave boys are winning!"
      in his cassock which could double as a dress.

The lame headmistress, Miss Dart, called by people Oppy Fart,
sings in her Sunday contralto voice.
      (Where is it hidden during the week?)

Mam takes him to town
to see sailor's collars bigger than sails.
      Here come the Yanks!

A Black Yank Soldier
outside a shop eating fish-'n-chips.
    Chips are built from spuds, hardly any fish.

Shouldn't say *spuds*.
The lame headmistress
    says, "Say *potatoes*."

As for fish,
they stay under the Atlantic,
    to detonate torpedoes.

Quentin Crisp in Transport

In London in the fifties I'd loiter
and in the course of loitering
would wonder, "Is there anything marketable in me?"
And thus loitering, would come across a group
tormenting an individual.
The individual was Quentin Crisp.

In Chelsea (where Quentin lived),
tourists and passers-by would question—
"That crowd? What's happening?"
"—a bloke wearing makeup." "75 per cent a woman!"
"Likes a bit of how's-your-father-up-his-garden-path."
Thus was Quentin persecuted.
And famous for being persecuted, his wit came later.
His wit came last.

In America at the beginning of the 21st century, I'd saunter.
As I sauntered, I'd wonder,
"If there's nothing marketable in me,
is there something I can give?"
And thus sauntering, I wandered onto a slow bus down 5th Avenue.
And who should get on at the bus-stop near the library?
Quentin! Now known in America as a writer,
self-sufficient as a character in Vermeer, flaunting
the apparatus that renders him a fugitive entertainer,
a literary gem,
90 yrs. old, favored by gravity—
the bus jolts and equilibrium chooses him a seat.
As a terrestrial with extra rouge,
eye shadow, mascara, blue tint for the hair,
he shares himself without apology.
An exhibitionist never says "sorry"
unless embroiled in criminology.
What in the name of face powder is there to forgive?

All the bus hates him.
Hate on public transport starts with a snarl in the genitals.
This snarl then travels the spine
to pizz-fizzle out the projectile eyes
in a vaporous fog wherein prejudice thrives.

As I exit, I stop next to Quentin.
"Are you Quentin Crisp?"
"Yes."
"Congratulations."
"Thank you."
"You are an inspiration!"
Then more loudly—
"To a lot of people."

The snarl coagulates within the vertebrae as confusion reigns.
But there's no danger of septicemia.
Soon up their spine hate snakes again,
the same old same old same old hate.

I Was Eighteen Virginia Years

Written in collaboration with Walter Cox

I was eighteen Virginia years.
Met this guy who took me in his car,
took me to his house.

Started hanging out.
Seemed to like me.
Seemed to like what I had between my legs.
It kinda paid off.

"I got to keep you here for awhile."
Talked about getting me a car.
*"You can have all this house here.
Forget about your girl.
Come live with me.
Enjoy it."*

"Don't know how I make a decision 'bout that.
Even there, not one among all the men in the world,
can't buy me.
That's giving up your manhood in your family.
I choose not to.
I will be your friend.
I will come over here and we will do things together,
have a little freak show."

*"I want you to stay.
I want you to live here with me."*

"What about school?
I got to go back to school."

*"You can go to school from here.
I will damn well take you to school.
You never have to work.
You can work at my house."*

"Well, I choose not to."

He just got mad when my girl called.
Gave her the number and she called.

"You let this...
this...
call you at my house?"

"Look, that is my woman there."

"I'm your woman."

"No you ain't. You'za man.
I pay you respect too.
But she come first.
She was there before you."

Left him alone.
Stopped messing with him.
He disappeared.
Never been heard of.
He's a gospel singer,
has to be still in Virginia—
shout-singin' the gospel
in some house arranged neatly
along with ten or so others,
all with lawns.

Another guy's father
had a chicken-box take-out.
Not a Kentucky Chicken.
Like a pizza,
but a chicken-box place.

He was a nice person.

He was like the young Michael Jackson
with a beautiful face,
unbleached.
His Daddy wasn't in the restaurant much.
We had a good time.

He wanted me to stay too.
I told him 'No.'
He was gentle in his reply.

*"That's alright. As long as we can
see each other twice a week in my daddy's resturant,
you can eat anything you like."*

Which I did.
Cleaned up for him.
Didn't have to pay me.
Did it in my own good time.
We had a broom.

He was gay.
Fucked like a girl, hollered like a girl.
If he said a word, you thought you'd be talking to a girl.
His voice was real tender.
Was I solid enough?
Not only in my most important part—
was I solid enough in thought and deed?

He was solid.
When I got locked up
he brought me money.
He fixed a letter from his Daddy so they gave me *hours*—
something like a pass.

I was out for eight hours,
getting my shit off.
Didn't kiss
but touched and stroked.

He had a cute face
like Michael
except there was a look
of comfortable violence
under a veil of petals
which I'd take off.

Veil taken off
Comfortable violence
What a blessing
Veil on
Looked like Michael
Veil off

Violence
Comfort
Blessing
Veil on
Veil off
Eighteen Virginia Years.

Door Taps

Me and Parker
neighbors on the 9th floor of a New York City building
                     became partners in our sixties.
                     This relationship could have lasted
                     except I died when I was 73.

The morning of my decease,
Parker leaves his apartment to get a coffee.
                     He knocks on my door.
                     I'm dead, so don't answer.
                     The night before,
                     aware I was about to croak,
                     I'd shot the bolt
                     so people would think I was alive.

Parker, continuing his journey, goes to the elevator.
Others get in but he descends without a by-your-leave.
                     We'd said—whoever went first,
                     we'd allow the wires to snap,
                     get used to our own company
                     again.

Outside in the bedraggled summer
the maintenance man approaches.
                     Parker explains
                     "My friend is not answering.
                     His door's locked on the inside."

The maintenance man looks pleased.
"I'll call the police."
                     He's never liked me
                     but we fucked frequently.
                     He fosters hate on all things
                     singularly—
                     a queer, a wreath, a friend, a grave.

Parker collects two shirts from the laundry,
walks two blocks to the Italian Lady for an iced coffee.
                     He's from North Carolina.
                     Black, gnarled and gristled,
                     he walks with a Carolina gait.

He opens a sidewalk container
to get the *Village Voice*,
>	obtains his copy.
>	With panache the Italian woman
>	adds ice to coffee—
>	trimmed panache, not too sweet.

Back in front of the building
>	ambulance
>	police cars
>	police with police forms.
>	Seniors from the building
>	white-faced, shaking.

Parker goes up in the elevator, unperplexed.
On the 9th he speaks to my doorway—
>	"The police and maintenance guy
>	are coming up in the elevator.
>	Separate from your corpse.
>	Let's say goodbye.
>	Make things complete."
>	I pass right through the door.
>	Advance into death in unfamiliar
>	gears,
>	no forward, no neutral, no retreat.

In the hall I follow Parker to his apartment.
He fixes a chair to keep his door open.
>	Back along the hall,
>	William the maintenance man
>	is banging on my door—
>	SLAM WRANG—.
>	He still dislikes me.
>	But the world doesn't worry.
>	He can fuck old men
>	as long as he demonstrates strength
>	with hate.

In the course of after-death communication
I ask Parker,
>	"What's in *The Voice*?"
>	"Another Tarantino Movie.
>	And Lena Horne passed.

>   Perhaps you'll meet."
>   —SLAM WRANG—
>   wails William the maintenance man
>   along the hallway.
>   *"I'M TAKING DOWN YOUR DOOR.
>   I'M HERE WITH THE POLICE."*
>   I tell Parker,
>   "You won't believe this...
>   I let the maintenance man do me.
>   Doo-diddle-hai me. In all positions."
>   My words register everywhere.
>   Especially on Parker's face

Gravity, getting feebler, is the present telling me,
"I have never been distinct."
>   With my door off its hinges,
>   police & paramedics
>   & the maintenance guy enter
>   while I give Parker one last kiss.
>   No sensation.
>   I've left already. I've already left . . .

left the torrent which is the hallway
for calm water which is the stairs
>   but on the stairs
>   can't tell banister from the stairwell
>   no difference between
>   windmill wind wind-sail
>   between the continuous never
>   the remembered nothing
>   the misplaced next.

About the Author

John Marcus Powell is a poet who is also an actor. Born in Wales, he has lived in London, Paris, Rome, Algeria, and for the past twenty-five years in New York City. His career as an actor spans British Rep, British soaps (as a doctor on ITV's Emergency Ward 10), American horror movies (Metamorphosis: The Alien Factor), London's West-End (Zigger-Zagger& Ian McKellan's understudy in The Promise), Off-Broadway (The Comedians& Perfect Crime), and Off-Off-Broadway (Hedda Gabler& The Visit). He was directed by Harold Pinter in Robert Shaw's The Man In The Glass Booth in London. Pinter encouraged his writing and helped him get his short stories published in Joe McCrindle's Transatlantic Review. He is the author of the chapbook, Loonie Lovers (Exot Books, 2012), and a full length collection of poems, Glorious Babe (Exot Books, 2014). He continues to perform his poetry extensively in New York City. As a poet he tap-dances to the rhythms of verse and prose, boogies through transgression, jives with socialism, square-dances with queerness, and flirts with any anarchic poet he's ever met—particularly Whitman, Shakespeare, Rimbaud, and Dickenson.

OTHER TITLES AVAILABLE FROM EXOT BOOKS

Schnauzer, David Yezzi ~ 2018
A Special Education, Meredith Bergmann ~ 2014
Glorious Babe, John Marcus Powell ~ 2014
Questions, Richard Loranger/Bill Mercer ~ 2013
Turn, Ann Drysdale ~ 2013
Tomorrow & Tomorrow, David Yezzi ~ 2013
Facing The Remains, Tom Merrill ~ 2012
Blue Wins Forever, Paco Brown ~ 2012
They Can Keep The Cinderblock, Mike Lane ~ 2012
Colors, Jay Chollick ~ 2011
Loony Lovers, John Marcus Powell ~ 2011
Filled With Breath: 30 Sonnets by 30 Poets, ed. Mary Meriam ~ 2010
Let Me Be Like Glass, Adriana Scopino ~ 2010
What's That Supposed To Mean, Wendy Videlock ~ 2010
We Internet In Different Voices, Mike Alexander ~ 2009
11 Films, Jane Ormerod ~ 2008
Aquinas Flinched, Rick Mullin ~ 2008
Graceways, Austin MacRae ~ 2008
Prospero At Breakfast, Alan Wickes ~ 2008
Sometime Before The Bell, Ray Pospisil ~ 2006
The Countess Of Flatbroke, Mary Meriam ~ 2006
Blue Glass Cities, Mark Allinson ~ 2006
Prolegomena To An Essay On Satire, R. Nemo Hill ~2006
William Montgomery, Quincy R. Lehr ~ 2006

ORDER ONLINE AT ~www.exottreasures.com/exotbooks

www.ingramcontent.com/pod-product-compliance
Lightning Source LLC
Chambersburg PA
CBHW030450010526
44118CB00011B/863